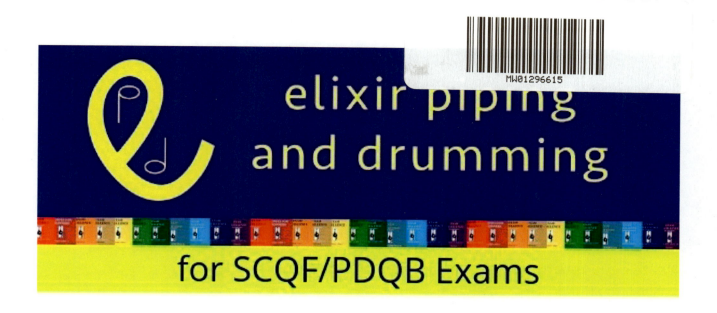

www.elixir.scot

Exam Excellence Task Books

Sight Reading Programme

Free Online Theory Games

Theory Practice Papers

Recordings

Great tools for both teacher and student

Excellence for Everyone

CHANTERS FOR CHILDREN

Copyright © 2018 Elixir Piping and Drumming
www.elixir.scot

ISBN: 978- 1544063560

All rights reserved
No part of this publication may be reproduced or transmitted in any form or by any means; electronic, mechanical, photocopying, recording, or otherwise, without the prior permission of the copyright owner.

A catalogue record for this book is available from the British Library

ALL TITLES FROM ELIXIR PIPING AND DRUMMING:

Chanters for Children
Bagpipes For Beginners *The Drummers Launch Pad*
Exam Repertoire Study Units 2 – 6
Study Unit 2 For Solo Pipers *Study Unit 2 For Pipe Band Drummers*
Study Unit 3 For Solo Pipers *Study Unit 3 For Pipe Band Drummers*
Study Unit 4 For Solo Pipers *Study Unit 4 For Pipe Band Drummers*
Study Unit 5 For Solo Pipers *Teaching Unit 1/Lesson Diary 1*
Study Unit 6 For Solo Pipers *Teaching Unit 2/Lesson Diary 2*
Study Unit 7 For Solo Pipers
Study Unit 8 For Solo Pipers
Study Unit 9 For Solo Pipers
Study Unit 10 For Solo Pipers *Sight Reading, Study Unit 1*
Study Unit 11 For Solo Pipers *Sight Reading, Study Unit 2*
Performance Unit 1 *Sight Reading, Study Unit 3*
Performance Unit 2 *Sight Reading, Study Unit 4*
Performance Unit 3 *Sight Reading, Study Unit 5*
Piobaireachd Unit *Sight Reading, Study Unit 6*
Teaching Unit 1/Lesson Diary 1 *Sight Reading, Study Unit 7*
Teaching Unit 2/Lesson Diary 2 *Sight Reading, Study Unit 8*

EXAM EXCELLENCE PROGRAMME

Chanters for Children

By Elixir Piping And Drumming

Suggested Teaching Schedule

Course Introduction Date: A / NA	Lesson 1 Date: A / NA	Lesson 2 Date: A / NA	Lesson 3 Date: A / NA	Lesson 4 Date: A / NA
Lesson 5 Date: A / NA	Revision Lesson Date: A / NA	Lesson 6 Date: A / NA	Lesson 7 Date: A / NA	Lesson 8 Date: A / NA
Lesson 9 Date: A / NA	Revision Lesson Date: A / NA	Lesson 10 Date: A / NA	Revision Lesson Date: A / NA	Lesson 11 Date: A / NA

**Suggested Teaching Schedule*
15x ½ hour lessons, TOTAL 7 ½ hours
THIS DOES NOT INCLUDE REQUIRED HOMEWORK TASKS AND INDIVIDUAL PRACTICE TIME

CONTENTS

Page	Study Area		A/NA
1	**PERFORMANCE**		
3	SA1	Blowing Skills	
5	SA2	Technique	
13	SA3	Sight Reading	
18	SA4	Repertoire	
20	**THEORY**		
22	SA1	Music Notation	
27	SA2	Instrument Care and Maintenance	
30	**EXAM EXCELLENCE**		

"Everything is Practice" — *Pele*

- Excellence is not a Gift, **Excellence is Practice**
- Practice does not make Perfect – **Practice makes Habit**
- Bad Practice = **Bad Habit = Bad Playing**
- Good Practice = **Good Habit = Good Playing**

Become What You Practice

THE ICEBERG *(The Secret of Success)*

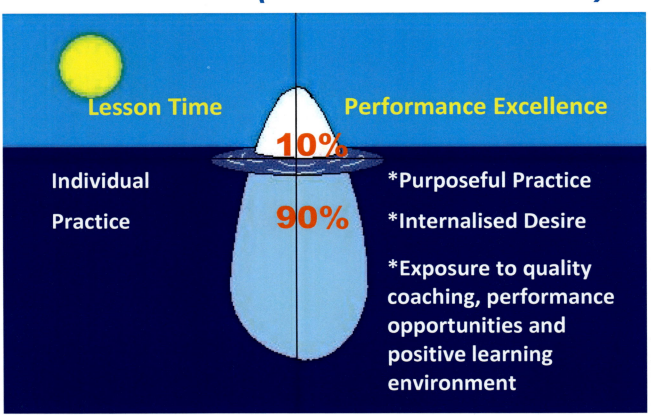

Lesson Time — **10%**

Performance Excellence

Individual Practice — **90%**

- *Purposeful Practice
- *Internalised Desire
- *Exposure to quality coaching, performance opportunities and positive learning environment

Performance

Page	Study Area	A/NA
3	**Blowing Skills**	
5	**Technique**	
13	**Sight Reading**	
18	**Repertoire**	

PERFORMANCE
PROGRESS CHART

TASK	Remarks	A/NA
Blowing Skills		
Hitting Rock Bottom		
The Only Way is UP		
Daily Workout		
Sight Reading		
Repertoire		

STUDY AREA 1 – BLOWING SKILLS

LESSON 1   LET'S BLOW!

TASK   **Breathing Exercise**

- **After the count of 2**, take a **deep breath**
- Hold for the **count of 10**
- **Release**

- **After the count of 2**, take a **deep breath**
- Hold for the **count of 10**
- **Release** under control for the **count of 10**

TASK   **Let's Blow!**

- Hold **chanter to mouth** with right hand (don't worry about covering any holes)
- **After the count of 2**, take a **deep breath**
- **Blow** chanter as long as possible

Groups - who can blow longest?

TASK   **Ready Steady Blow!**

Ready	Place chanters in **ready to blow** position
1.	
2.	Take a **deep breath**
3.	**Blow**
And	**Warning** – prepare to stop
Stop	Clean **finish**

Outcome
Controlled deep breathing technique from the diaphragm

CHANTERS FOR CHILDREN

STUDY AREA 1 – BLOWING SKILLS
WHAT'S HOT, WHAT'S NOT

Introduction to Blowing Pressure

Blow a steady and sustained sound . . . "HOT" or "NOT"?

HOT – steady and sustained sound

NOT – wavering sound *(dropping pressure)*

      - cutting out *(over blowing)*

      - croaky sound *(under blowing)*

TASK	Steady as you Blow
Ready	Place chanters in **ready to blow** position
1.	
2.	Take a **deep breath**
3.	**Blow** a steady and constant blowing pressure
And	**Warning** – prepare to stop
Stop	Clean **finish**

Outcome
Controlled blowing pressure producing a steady and constant sound

STUDY AREA 2 - TECHNIQUE

LESSON 2   HITTING ROCK BOTTOM – LOW G

The Bagpipe Scale

There are **2 G's and A's** -

identified as *High* or *Low*

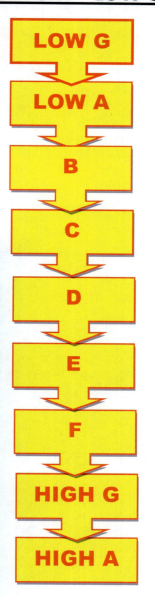

TASK	LOW G – Bottom Note

Top Hand –

- Place left hand thumb on back hole
- Cover holes with each finger in turn leaving little finger (pinky) free

Bottom Hand –

- Place little finger *(pinky)* on the bottom hole
- Cover holes with each finger in turn
- Rest your thumb on the back of the chanter
- Sound Low G, practice as required

*All fingers should be straight – use the pads of your fingers rather than the tips

Outcome
Sound Low G with correct finger positions

STUDY AREA 2 - TECHNIQUE
HITTING ROCK BOTTOM – G FORCE

TASK **3 in a Row**

- Sound a **long low G**
- Place the **chanter on the table** *(hands clear)*
- **Repeat** as required *(3 correct Low G's in a row)*

TASK **10 Down**

- Start with **chanter on table** *(hands clear)*
- Count of 10 – lift chanter, place **fingers on Low G** position
- **Sound Low G** *(count of 10)*
- Place **chanter on table** *(hands clear)*

- Count of 9 – lift chanter, place **fingers on Low G** position
- **Sound Low G** *(count of 9)*
- Place **chanter on table** *(hands clear)*

Repeat from 10 down to 1

Outcome
Consistently sound Low G with correct finger positions
Developed hand and finger positioning

STUDY AREA 2 - TECHNIQUE
LESSON 3   THE ONLY WAY IS UP – BOTTOM HAND SCALE

TASK   **Bottom Hand Scale**

- **Sound Low G**
- **Sound Low A** - Lift Bottom finger *(Low A finger)*
- **Sound B** - Lift next finger *(B finger)*
- **Sound C** - lift next finger *(C finger)* and replace Low A finger
- **Sound D** - Lift next finger *(D finger)* leaving Low A finger down

TASK

On the count in, play together:

2/4   ‖   **LG   LA | B   C | D   D** ‖

Outcome
Play bottom hand scale

STUDY AREA 2 - TECHNIQUE

THE ONLY WAY IS UP   **BRIDGING THE GAP (D to E)**

TASK   **Sound E**

- **Sound D**
- **Sound E**   – top hand - lift 1st finger *(E finger)*
                – bottom hand - Low A

TASK   **Call out the Emergency Services (D, E, D, E, D, E)**
Practice   D → E → D

TASK

On the count in, play together:

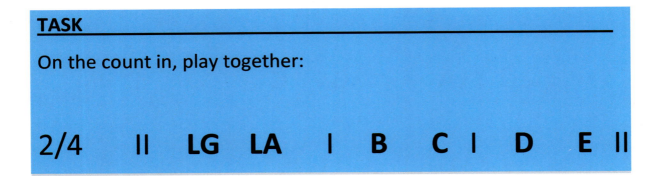

Outcome
Correctly bridge the gap from D to E

STUDY AREA 2 - TECHNIQUE

THE ONLY WAY IS UP   TOP HAND SCALE

Top Hand Scale

*For E, F, High G and High A always **keep bottom hand on Low A***

- **Sound E**
- **Sound F** - Lift next finger *(F finger)*
- **Sound High G** - Lift top finger *(High G finger)*
- **Sound High A** – Lift thumb and lower E finger

TASK

On the count in, play together *(bottom hand Low A position)*:

3/4   ‖   E   F   G' | A'   A'   A'   ‖

Outcome
Play top hand scale

CHANTERS FOR CHILDREN

STUDY AREA 2 - TECHNIQUE

THE ONLY WAY IS UP   **ALL 9 NOTES**

The Bagpipe Scale

TASK
On the count in, play together:

2/4 ‖ LG LA | B C | D E |

| F G' | A' A' ‖

TASK – Play It Say It Quiz   (Note Recognition)

Play and Say for points, split into teams or beat the teacher

- **Play it** (Instructor plays the note)   **Say it** (Student names the note)
- **Say it** (Instructor says the note)   **Play it** (Student plays the note)

Remember!
- **Correct** finger positions
- **Straight** fingers
- **Clean** changeovers *(no crossing noises)*
- **Think** before you play *(know the notes)*

Outcome
Correctly play the full bagpipe scale

Note Recognition

STUDY AREA 2 - TECHNIQUE

LESSON 4   DAILY WORKOUT

Grace notes are short notes played quickly before a melody note.

They are written smaller than a normal note on the page

Gracenote tails go up,

and melody note tails go down

We practice technique to strengthen hands and develop co-ordination

Required Outcome
Daily Workout to be played:
- Correct
- Clean
- Together
- 1 breath per exercise

Practice Protocols
- **Ready:** Hands on chanter *(1st finger position)*
- **Inhale** after count and **play on next beat**
- **Play full exercise** in one complete breath *(if possible)*
- Beat time, **play to the beat** *(steady + controlled)*
- Give all notes their **full value**
- **Clean finish**, hands on chanter, **ready for next** exercise

TASK
Practice and master the Daily Workout

Introduction to Technique

1. The Scale

2. Scale to F with G Gracenote

3. Gracenote Exercise - Minims

4. Gracenote Exercise - Crotchets

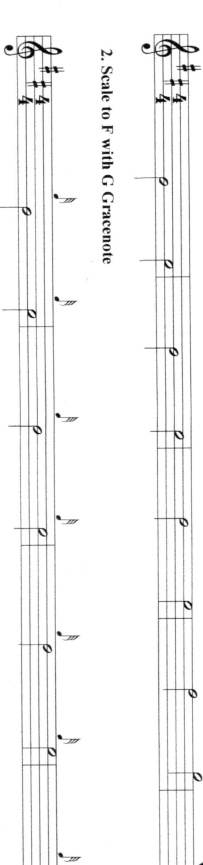

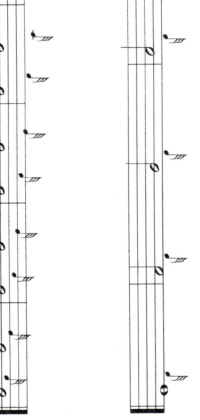
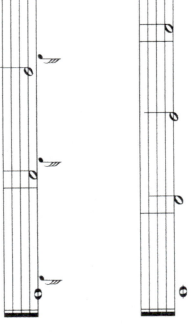

Outcome

Basic knowledge and understanding, and correct playing of introductory technique exercises

STUDY AREA 3 – SIGHT READING
INTRODUCTION TO SIGHT READING

1. LOOK, THINK, SAY

Before playing:

- **Look** at each note
- **Think** what it is called
- **Say** the name out loud

NOTE:
Students are advised at this point to study the theory section before returning to sight reading.

2. LOOK, THINK, PLAY

- **Look** at the note
- **Think** how it is played
- **Play** the note

Reading and playing music takes **practice**.
Be patient, the more you practice the easier it will become.

TASK
Study and play the following examples

Outcome
Knowledge, understanding and practice of basic sight reading skills

STUDY AREA 3 – SIGHT READING

1.

2.

3.

4.

5.

6.

7.

8.

Outcome
Knowledge, understanding and practice of basic sight reading skills

STUDY AREA 3 – SIGHT READING

1.

2.

3.

4.

Outcome

Knowledge, understanding and practice of basic sight reading skills

STUDY AREA 3 – SIGHT READING

Outcome
Knowledge, understanding and practice of basic sight reading skills

STUDY AREA 3 – SIGHT READING

1.

2.

3.

4.

Outcome
Knowledge, understanding and practice of basic sight reading skills

STUDY AREA 4 – REPERTOIRE

LESSON 5   **EFFECTIVE PRACTICE**

10 minutes EFFECTIVE PRACTICE is better than 10 hours practicing mistakes

Effective Practice   **(Become What You Practice)**

1. **Sight Reading**
   - *Look, think, say*: correctly identify all notes and grace notes
   - *Look, think, play*: correctly play all notes and grace notes

2. **Mastering**
   - Practice until playing exactly as written *(phrase by phrase)*
   - Pay special attention to gracing and timing *(note length)*
   - Practicing what you're good at keeps you the same, practicing what you're bad at makes you better
     - fix mistakes, don't repeat them

3. **Memorising**
   - Repetitious practice *(phrase by phrase)* until correct from memory

TASK
Learn and play selected piece correct from memory

Outcome
Knowledge and understanding of effective practice, learning and memorising technique
Play a piece of music correct from memory

Sunset

Slow Air

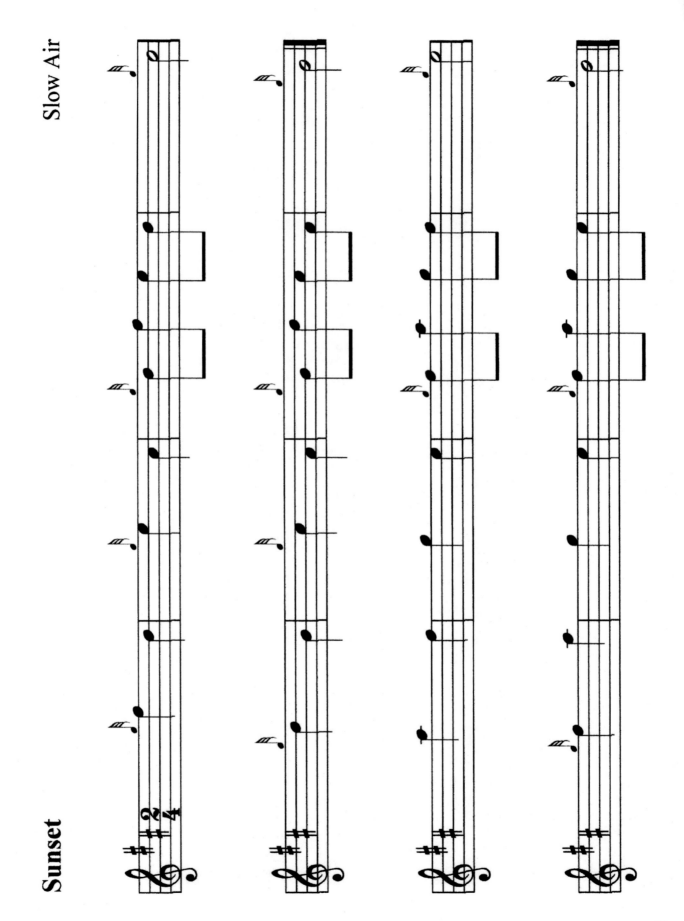

CHANTERS FOR CHILDREN

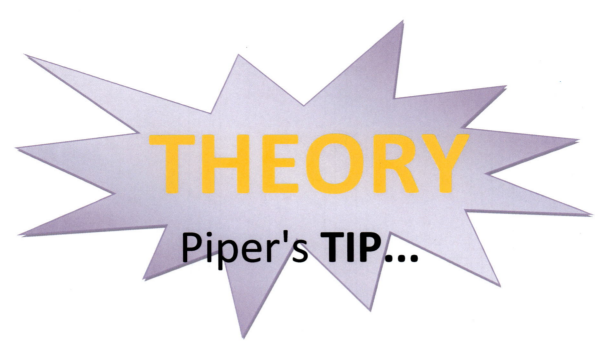

THEORY
Piper's TIP...

Theory

Improves

Playing

All theory tasks are recommended as homework, to make effective use of lesson time

A music manuscript book is recommended for additional practice

Page		A/NA
22	**Music Notation**	
27	**Instrument Care and Maintenance**	

THEORY

PROGRESS CHART

TASK	Remarks	A/NA
Reading the Stave		
Reading the Notes		
Note Value Table		
Instrument Care and Maintenance		

STUDY AREA 1 – MUSIC NOTATION

LESSON 6   **READING THE STAVE**

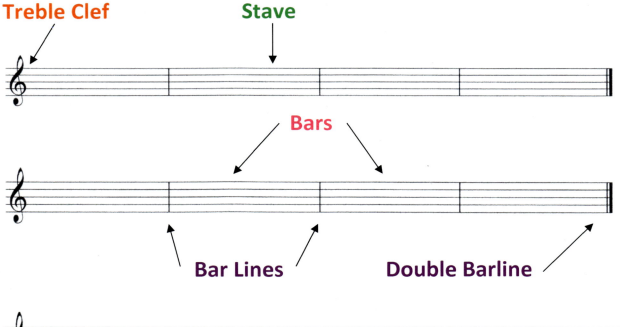

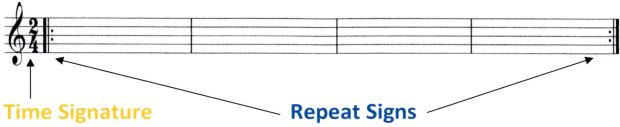

- **Stave** - 5 lines music is written on
- **Treble Clef** - Starts every line
- **Bar Lines** - Split the stave into equal sections
- **Bars** – The name for these sections
- **Double Bar Line** – Ends the section
- **Repeat Sign** - Two dots with a double bar line
- **Time Signature** - The two numbers at the start

Outcome
Introduction to music notation

STUDY AREA 1 – MUSIC NOTATION

READING THE NOTES

The notes on the bagpipes are:

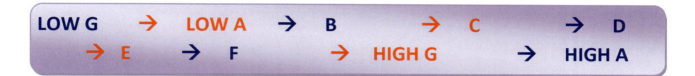

To help recognise the notes on the stave:
- Hold out your top hand *(usually left),* with thumb on top/palm facing
- Your 5 fingers are now the lines of the stave

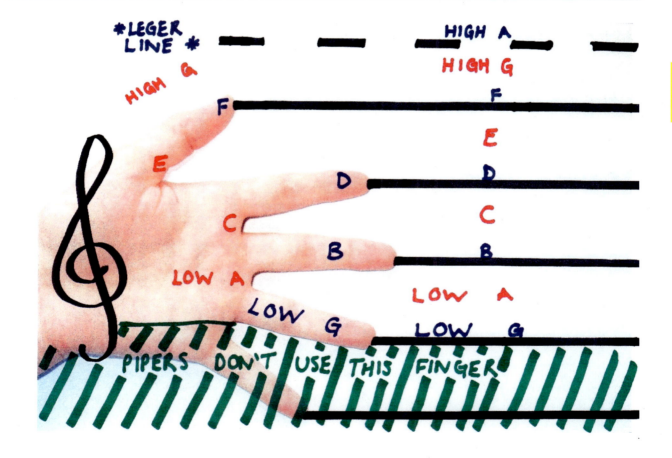

Outcome
Correctly identify notes on the stave

CHANTERS FOR CHILDREN

TASK — Say It Play It
Say the name of the note, then play it on the chanter

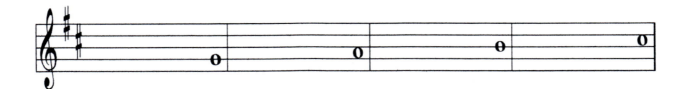

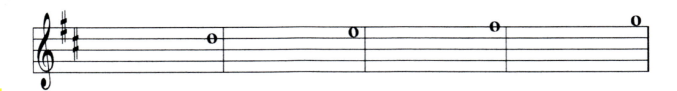

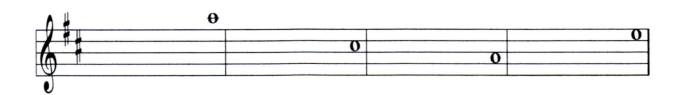

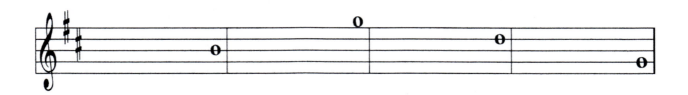

Outcome
Note Recognition

STUDY AREA 1 – MUSIC NOTATION

LESSON 7   **NOTE VALUE TABLE**

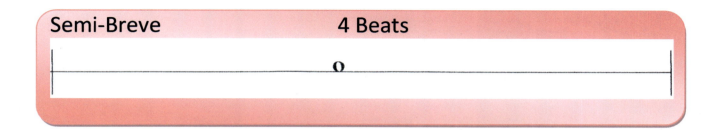

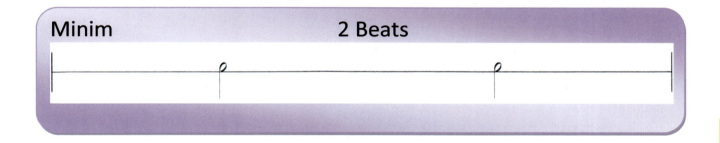

Outcome
Understanding Note Values

CHANTERS FOR CHILDREN

TASK   Say It Play It

Say the name of the note, number of beats, and play it on the chanter

Outcome
Note Recognition and Note Values

STUDY AREA 2 – INSTRUMENT CARE AND MAINTENANCE

LESSON 9   PRACTICE CHANTER MAINTENANCE

Safely Dismantling the Practice Chanter After Playing

- Use both hands to grip chanter bowl and ferrule
- Turn with care and lift straight off
- Do not turn chanter from the bottom as this may damage or break chanter
- Take care not to damage reed blades

Clean and Dry After Playing

- Shake off excess moisture
- Remove reed, leave to dry
- Brush mouthpiece

Hemping

- Use waxed hemp
- It is water resistant
- It produces an airtight seal
- Wind hemp evenly under tension
- Check as you go for good fit

Outcome
Knowledge and understanding of practice chanter maintenance

STUDY AREA 2 – INSTRUMENT CARE AND MAINTENANCE
TROUBLE SHOOTING

Problem – Blowing but no sound

Cause 1 – Over blowing

Solution – Reduce blowing pressure

Cause 2 – Dislodged reed

Solution A – Gently shake reed into position

Solution B – Separate chanter and replace reed

Problem – Wavering Sound

Cause – Unsteady blowing

Solution – Blow a full and steady pressure

Problem – Unable to separate practice chanter

Cause – Blowing moisture (hemp has expanded)

Solution A – Use a piece of leather for better grip

Solution B – Leave to dry (hemp will contract)

Problem – Chanter too Loose

Cause – Lack of practice

Solution – Hemp mid-section

Outcome
Knowledge and understanding in instrument fault checking

STUDY AREA 2 – INSTRUMENT CARE AND MAINTENANCE

ORAL TASK

TASK	A/NA
Explain and demonstrate how to safely dismantle the practice chanter **(4)**	
Explain and demonstrate how to clean and dry practice chanter after playing **(3)**	
Explain and demonstrate correct hemping technique **(5)**	

Outcome
Knowledge and understanding of practice chanter maintenance

Exam Excellence

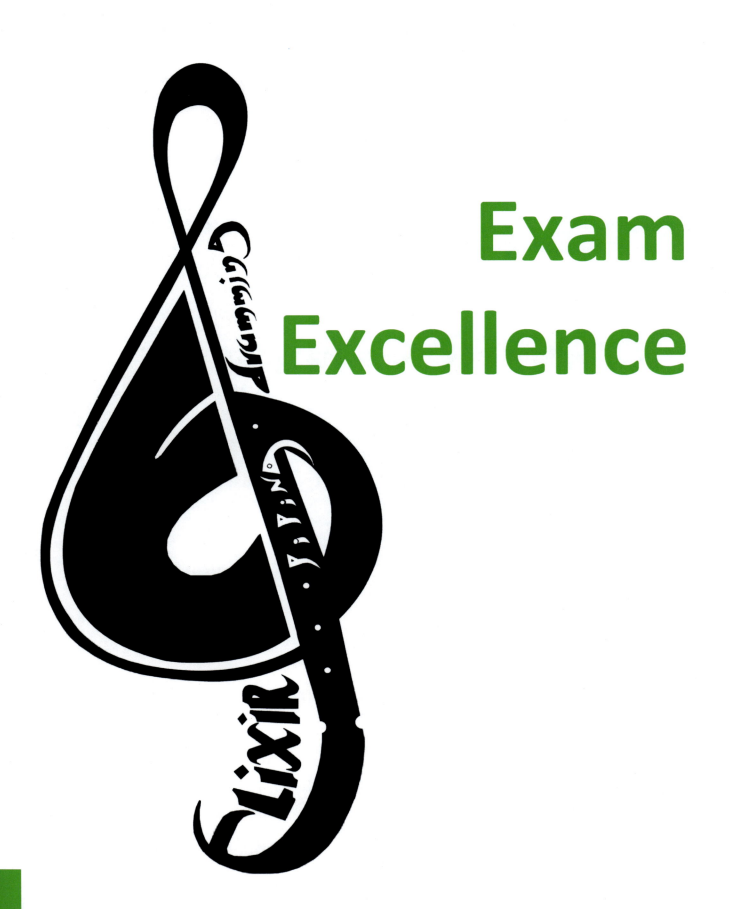

EXAM EXCELLENCE

LESSON 10   PERFORMANCE PRACTICE

FINAL TASK

- Answer **instrument care and maintenance** questions

- Perform **technique** on **practice chanter**

    (correct from memory)

- Perform **exam repertoire** on the **practice chanter**

    (correct from memory)

CHANTERS FOR CHILDREN

EXAM EXCELLENCE

LESSON 11 — PERFORMANCE

TECHNIQUE	A/NA
Scale	
Scale to F with G Gracenote	
Gracenote Exercise – Minims	
Gracenote Exercise - Crotchets	
Remarks	

CARE AND MAINTENANCE Explain and demonstrate the following:	A/NA
Safely dismantle practice chanter	
Clean and dry practice chanter after playing	
Hemping technique	
Remarks	

SLOW AIR	A/NA
Remarks	

EXAM EXCELLENCE

STUDENT RECORD

Date	Study Area	Complete/Remarks	A/NA
	PERFORMANCE		
	1. Blowing Skills		
	2. Technique		
	3. Sight reading		
	4. Repertoire		
	THEORY		
	1. Music Notation		
	2. Maintenance		

Name:_____   All Study Areas: A / NA____

Date:_____   Signed:_____

This certifies that

_____

Has successfully completed

Chanters for Children

Kick Start Programme

Well Done!

Signed: _____ Date: _____

Made in the USA
Columbia, SC
07 March 2019